Sam Houston

Carolyn Turner

WEIGL PUBLISHERS INC.
"Creating Inspired Learning"
www.weigl.com

Published by Weigl Publishers Inc.
350 5th Avenue, 59th Floor
New York, NY 10118
Website: www.weigl.com

Library of Congress Cataloging-in-Publication Data

Turner, Carolyn, 1948-
 Sam Houston : my life / Carolyn Turner.
     p. cm.
 Includes index.
 ISBN 978-1-61690-065-6 (alk. paper) -- ISBN 978-1-61690-066-3 (softcover : alk. paper) -- ISBN 978-1-60596-941-1 (e-book)
 1. Houston, Sam, 1793-1863--Juvenile literature. 2. Governors--Texas--Biography--Juvenile literature. 3. Legislators--United States--Biography--Juvenile literature. 4. United States. Congress. Senate--Biography--Juvenile literature. 5. Texas--History--To 1846--Juvenile literature. I. Title.
 F390.H84T87 2010
 976.4'04092--dc22
 [B]
                                   2010005478

Printed in the United States of America in North Mankato, Minnesota
1 2 3 4 5 6 7 8 9 0 14 13 12 11 10

042010
WEP264000

Editor: Heather C. Hudak   **Design**: Kenzie Browne

All of the Internet URLs given in the book were valid at the time of publication. However, due to the dynamic nature of the Internet, some addresses may have changed, or sites may have ceased to exist since publication. While the author and publisher regret any inconvenience this may cause readers, no responsibility for any such changes can be accepted by either the author or the publisher.

Every reasonable effort has been made to trace ownership and to obtain permission to reprint copyright material. The publishers would be pleased to have any errors or omissions brought to their attention so that they may be corrected in subsequent printings.

Weigl acknowledges Getty Images as its primary image supplier for this title.

CONTENTS

Who is Sam Houston?

"Big" Sam Houston was an important person in Texas history. At one time, Texas was owned by Mexico. Houston led an important battle that helped the United States gain control of the state. Then, he became a politician. He did important work for the people of Texas.

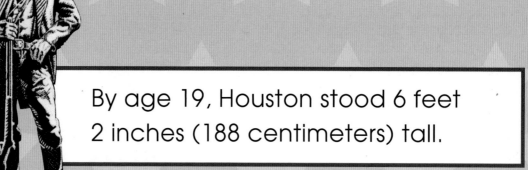

By age 19, Houston stood 6 feet 2 inches (188 centimeters) tall.

Growing Up

Houston was born in Virginia on March 2, 1793. He had five brothers and three sisters.

Houston's father, Samuel, was an army major. He died when Houston was 14 years old. Houston's mother, Elizabeth, moved the family to Maryville, Tennessee.

Houston loved to read. He was inspired by the many books he read. *The Iliad* was one of his favorites.

All About Virginia

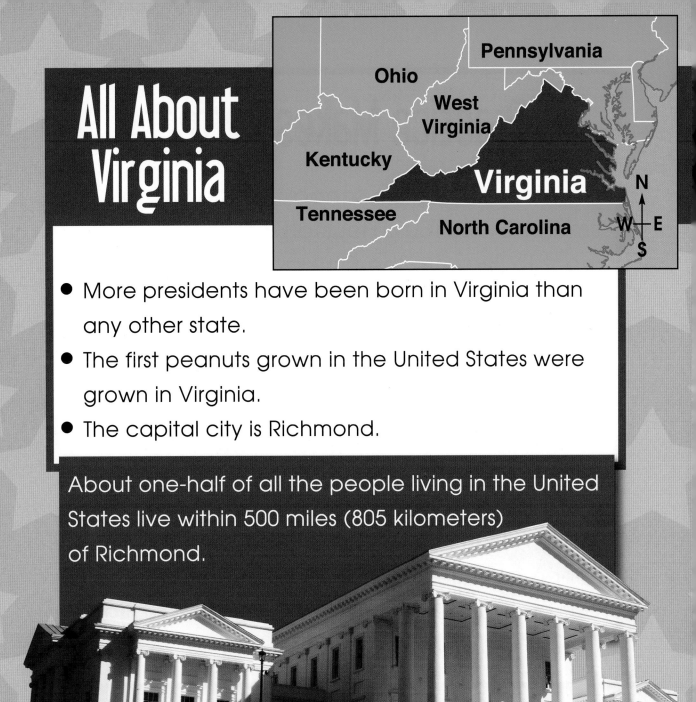

- More presidents have been born in Virginia than any other state.
- The first peanuts grown in the United States were grown in Virginia.
- The capital city is Richmond.

About one-half of all the people living in the United States live within 500 miles (805 kilometers) of Richmond.

Practice Makes Perfect

Houston did not like school, but he was a smart boy. In 1809, Houston left school and went to live with the Cherokee Indians.

Houston loved adventure. In 1813, he joined the army. Houston did well and quickly was made an officer. By 1819, Houston had left the army to become a lawyer. He then served as a **congressman** for two terms.

In 1827, Houston became the governor of Tennessee. He left this job two years later to become a member of the Cherokee Nation. He moved to Texas in 1832.

9

Influences

Houston was influenced by the Cherokee Indians. He learned their language and ways of life. He even dressed in traditional Cherokee clothing. Chief Oolooteka gave Houston an Indian name. He called Houston *Colonneh*, or "Raven."

Houston admired how his mother raised eight children on her own. Like his mother, Houston worked hard and had strong goals.

Houston served under Andrew Jackson in the army. Jackson was a **military** leader who later became president. He helped Houston become a **representative** to the Cherokee.

11

Key Events

In 1833, Houston set up a law **practice** in Nacogdoches, Texas. He became the commanding general of the Army of the **Republic of Texas** in 1836. Soon after, Houston led Texas against Mexico in the **Battle of San Jacinto**. Texas was freed, and Houston became a hero to the people of Texas.

Houston became the first president of the Republic of Texas in 1836. He served in the position until 1838.

In 1841, Houston began a second term as president of the Republic of Texas. This term ended in 1844.

In 1846, Houston was elected to the U.S. Senate. He served in this position until 1859.

Houston became governor of Texas in 1859. He is the only person in U.S. history to serve as governor in two different states.

Overcoming Obstacles

Houston faced challenges in the army. He was shot in the leg with an arrow during the **Battle of Horseshoe Bend** in 1814. Houston had the arrow pulled out and kept fighting. Later, two bullets struck his upper body. Many people thought Houston would die. He was strong and survived the wounds.

Some states no longer wanted to be part of the United States. As governor, Houston did not want Texas to leave the **Union**. He made speeches about his views. Some people did not agree with him, and he lost his position as governor. Houston continued to stand by his beliefs.

15

Achievements and Successes

Houston is best remembered as a strong leader. The people of Texas have not forgotten how he helped their state gain its freedom. There are reminders of Houston's achievements all over Texas.

There is a Sam Houston memorial in Houston, Texas.

The world's largest statue of a U.S. hero is of Sam Houston. It is in Huntsville, Texas.

The USS *Sam Houston* was a world-class submarine named after Houston.

The Sam Houston State University is in Huntsville, Texas. It was founded in 1879 and is one of the oldest universities in Texas.

The city of Houston, Texas, is named after Sam Houston.

What is a Politician?

Politicians are people who are elected to government jobs. They represent the people who vote for them and make decisions on behalf of these people. Politicians help make laws. They try to find ways to make cities, states, and countries better places to live.

Politicians Through History

Like Houston, these politicians have had great success.

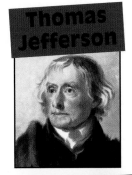

Thomas Jefferson

Thomas Jefferson wrote the Declaration of Independence. This document stands for the United States' **ideals** of freedom and **democracy**.

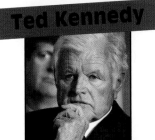

Ted Kennedy

Kennedy became a senator in 1962. He served for nearly 47 years. When he died in 2009, only two other senators had served longer.

Barack Obama

On January 20, 2009, Obama became the first African American U.S. president.

Timeline

1793	Sam Houston was born on March 2 in Virginia.
1818	Houston began to study law.

1827 | Houston was elected governor of Tennessee.

1836 | Houston was elected the first president of the Republic of Texas.

1846 | Houston became senator of Texas.

1859 | Houston was elected governor of Texas.

1863 | Houston died of **pneumonia**. He was buried in Huntsville, Texas.

Write a Biography

A person's life story can be the subject of a book. This kind of book is called a biography. Biographies describe the lives of people who have had great success or done important things to help others. These people may be alive today, or they may have lived many years ago.

Try writing your own biography. First, decide who you want to write about. You can choose a politician, such as Sam Houston, or any other person you find interesting. Then, find out if your library has any books about this person.

Write down the key events in this person's life.

- What was this person's childhood like?
- What has he or she accomplished?
- What are his or her goals?
- What makes this person special or unusual?

Answer the questions in your notebook. Your answers will help you write your biography review.

Find Out More

To learn more about Sam Houston, visit these websites.

Visit this site for information about Sam Houston.
www.pbs.org/weta/thewest/
people/d_h/houston.htm

Check out this site to learn about the life of Sam Houston.
www.tsl.state.tx.us/treasures/giants/houston-01.html

Find out about San Jacinto Day at this site.
www.timeanddate.com/
holidays/us/san-jacinto-day

Find out more about the life and work of Sam Houston.
www.lone-star.net/mail/
texasinfo/shouston.htm

Lone Star Internet

Business Solutions
Lone Star Mall
Culture Cafe
Texas Trails
Site Index
Search

Where business happe

Sam Houston "The Raven" (1793-1863)

info, trivia and actual quotes.....

Sam(uel) Houston, governor of two states, president of the Republic of Texas, U.S. senator, and military hero, was one of the most colorful figures of 19th-century America. Born near Lexington, Va., on Mar. 2, 1793, he was reared in Tennessee by his widowed mother. As a youth he spent much time with Cherokee Indians and developed close ties with them. Joining the army, he served under Andrew Jackson in the Creek wars (1813-14). In 1818, Houston resigned his commission and, after studying law for a few months, was elected attorney general for Nashville and appointed adjutant general of Tennessee. He served two terms in Congress (1823-27) and in 1827 was elected governor of Tennessee.

While governor, Houston married Eliza Allen on Jan. 1, 1829. For unexplained reasons (see below), however, the marriage was dissolved almost immediately, and Houston, under pressure from the influential Allen family, resigned his office. For the next 6 years he lived with Cherokee Indians in the Indian Territory (now Oklahoma), taking a Cherokee wife, Tiana Rogers (see below), and adopting Cherokee citizenship. He was a trader, advisor, and special envoy for the tribe on several occasions. It was in this last capacity that he first went to Texas, then under Mexican rule, in 1832 in a futile attempt to secure a land grant for the tribe. By 1835, Houston had moved to Texas. With the outbreak of the Texas Revolution in that year he was named commanding general of the revolutionary army. In March 1836, Houston was a delegate to the convention that declared Texas an independent republic. His command was reconfirmed, and he led the Texas army to a brilliant victory over Santa Anna in the Battle of San Jacinto (Apr. 21, 1836).

Houston served as the first president of the new republic from 1836 to 1838 and was later elected to a second term (1841-44). After the annexation (1845) of Texas by the United States, he was elected to the U.S. Senate, serving from 1846 to 1859. In the Senate, Houston was known for his staunch Unionism and friendship for the Indians. Unhappy that Texas seemed to be moving toward secession, he successfully ran for governor as an independent Unionist in 1859. Despite his efforts, however, the people of Texas voted to secede, and he was forced out of office in March 1861.

In 1840, Houston had married Margaret Lea in Alabama. She had persuaded him to stop drinking, for which he had a sizeable reputation, and to join the Baptist church. They had eight children. Houston died at his home in Huntsville on July 26, 1863. The city of Houston, Texas, was named for him.

Glossary

Battle of Horseshoe Bend: a fight that took place in Alabama during the War of 1812

Battle of San Jacinto: a fight led by Sam Houston; it gave Texas independence from Mexico

congressman: a person who is a member of the U.S. Congress

democracy: a government system in which people vote for a person to speak on their behalf

ideals: concepts that are thought to be perfect

military: relating to soldiers or armed forces

pneumonia: a lung infection

practice: a place of business

representative: a person chosen to speak on behalf of other people

Republic of Texas: an independent country from 1836 to 1845

Union: the name given to the U.S. government during the Civil War; made up of 23 states

Index